PUT YOUR BEST SELF FORWARD

PALMETTO
P U B L I S H I N G
Charleston, SC
www.PalmettoPublishing.com

Copyright © 2024 by Anthony Snowdale

All rights reserved

No portion of this book may be reproduced, stored in a retrieval system, or transmitted in any form by any means–electronic, mechanical, photocopy, recording, or other–except for brief quotations in printed reviews, without prior permission of the author.

Paperback ISBN: 9798822959972

PUT YOUR BEST SELF FORWARD

HOW SMALL STEPS CAN
TAKE YOU BIG PLACES

Anthony Snowdale

DEDICATION

This book is dedicated to my mother. You are the kindest and most gentle soul I've known. Your love and support got me through the turbulence and turmoil of my youth. You were the extension ladder that rescued me from all the deep holes I dug. Your fight against the beast of cancer shows me what true valor looks like and inspires me to never take health for granted—to fight for it even harder for my clients, my family, and myself.

To my father, my dearest friend and most faithful health coaching client. Everything good that I've been able to build in my life has been on the bedrock that is my Dad. Your ever present unconditional love and support has been my compass, a safety net, and a valuable teacher throughout my years.

To my stepmother, Donna. For most of my life, you have been a positive force, teaching by example important things like balance, joy, empathy, and kindness. You are the best example I know of someone who seeks, finds, and draws out the best in others, a quality that I work to make my own.

To my angel from heaven, Talia. The sight of your gorgeous face lights me up with joy and gratitude. I'm so proud of the kind, compassionate, sweet, and hilarious person you're becoming. You are my most profound source of joy. As I always tell you, I am the luckiest Daddy ever to get to have you as a daughter.

To my son, Christian. You are my best buddy and my most valuable teacher. You were the person who first taught me to love on the deepest level. I couldn't be more proud of the young man you are growing into. Kind, generous, intelligent, handsome, athletic, gentle, funny and loving. All the things that I wish to be myself, you already are. As I whisper into your ear as you fall asleep each night, you are the best boy in the world.

To my beautiful wife. You are my everything. Your kindness, generosity, dedication to family, and hard work inspires me every day. You are the North Star for our brood, and we'd all be wandering around lost and naked without you. You are my best friend and the person who has allowed me to grow. You support me—always. You are the reason for my strength. You are the reason for my gentleness. You are the love of my life, and I'll cherish you forever.

To my friends, family, and clients. I love you all. You are all threads in the tapestry of my life. You make it beautiful. Thank you.

TABLE OF CONTENTS

Introduction 1
1 Backstory 5
2 Taking Responsibility 15
3 Word Becomes Flesh 21
4 Have a Target 29
5 Serve 37
6 Nutrition 43
7 Fasting 51
8 Move. Your. Body! 59
9 Meditation 71
10 The Beginning 81
About the Author 84

INTRODUCTION

Picture this book as words from a friend. One who is deeply concerned with your well-being and is in your corner completely. Someone who will rejoice in your successes and make battle plans against your struggles. Though we may have never met, I *do* care immensely about you. Your well-being. Your triumph. I *am* in your corner. I want to show you how you can get from where you are to where you want to go. This book will be a gentle nudge in that direction.

In this book you will learn actionable strategies for improving your health, learning how and when to move your body, deepening your relationships, developing determination, setting and achieving goals, and having a more meaningful and purposeful existence.

You'll learn how important it is to forever be a student. We never stop moving towards worthy ideals. We incrementally improve each day. We never stop learning. For, if this is your way, you'll one day look back down at the trail you've followed and realize just how impossibly far you've gone. You will then turn your eyes back to the summit and continue.

If you implement just one thing from this book, I promise that one thing will help you shape a better life. Take all you can from this book. All that speaks to you. Revisit it once in a while because the person re-reading this one year from now will be a different one. One who will take different things away.

Since you have this book in your hand, I know you're ready to *make* change. Change is coming no matter what. Change is the only constant. Be the curator of the changes ahead—master of them, not subject to them. It's time to completely take control of your thoughts, actions, and their subsequent outcomes. To shape the best life you can. To put your best self forward.

1

BACKSTORY

I was the most average person (or below in many cases) that ever lived. In my younger life, I was definitely not the fastest or most coordinated kid in gym class. Middling in all academic endeavors. Not ugly but not handsome. Had a few friends but was shy. Terrified to talk to girls. Had divorced parents and a few close family relationships but for sure no Ward, June, and the Beav close-knit family dynamic. Just about every other way you could gauge a kid's life, I'd be right in the middle.

This center of the herd trend continued all the way until junior high. It was then that my friend group and I started to dabble in drinking and smoking pot. It was also then when I distinguished myself as leader. You see, I'd found what I was good at. When the other kids were tipsy after a few beers, I was finishing my six pack (and everyone else's). When everyone was choking and coughing, I was smoking half a joint in one hit. It was the first time in my life I'd heard, "Wow, look at Tony go!" It was the first thing I was, well, really good at.

Being the best at drugs and alcohol was my defining characteristic through my teens and early twenties. Didn't matter what we were doing—coke, k, ecstasy—I was head and shoulders above everyone in tolerance. First to break it out. Last to put it down. I was legendary among my group, even a bit outside of it. It felt good for Mr. Average to be amazing at something. Being shy and talking to girls was no longer a problem after eight beers. Making new friends came easier too. The lack in my family relationships was numbed by substance, and who the hell cared about grades, anyway? Not me, so I dropped out of high school and went full time into the partying business—and boy, was it a boomin'.

As you might imagine, this way of life didn't lead to many good places. It wasn't long before even I realized that I was in a downward spiral. So I moved to California to start anew. Then, it wasn't long before I realized that the pharmacies twenty minutes away in Mexico sold all their wares without those pesky prescriptions. You see, no matter how far you run, you'll never get away from yourself. The one thing I learned in San Diego was that of the vast cornucopia of drugs available in the world, the ones that spoke the most to me were in the opioid family. So I took that knowledge back home to Boston and went pro in opiates.

Oxycontin was the thing back in those days. One dollar a milligram, and I could get off on $40! For the first week. My dosage (not so) slowly creeped up to two 80mg pills per day. Now at the time, I was making $150 a day as a roofer and spending $160 on drugs. I'm no mathematical genius or economist, but I did realize this was not a sustainable economic model. So I switched to heroin for financial purposes. *But* I made rules…and broke every one of them. Things like:

"I'll never spend more than $50 a day."
"Ok, no more than $100 a day."
"Well, I'll never inject. I'll only snort it."
"Ok, I'll inject but never share a needle."
"Well, I'll never share a needle with *that* guy"…

On and on I went. Until I became an empty shell of a person. Until the drug had no effect other than keeping me from being violently ill. I could trust nothing. Not my own word, and eventually not even the fact I'd be alive for long.

On my first bad overdose, I was brought back to life in the back of an ambulance with a shot of Narcan. If you don't know, it instantly flushes the drugs out of your system. This causes you, well, to not die. It also causes you to be instantly dope sick. I popped up and barked at the EMT, "Where's my jacket!?" Then I noticed my girlfriend at the time was there too. I saw her face switch from panic to angry disbelief to solemn determination to get away from me, all in seconds. I knew it was over. One more bridge torched. I was so sick that I didn't care at all. The only thing I cared about was getting more dope, and I did just that wearing jeans and a hospital Johnny.

My second bad OD was just a few days later, on my twenty-sixth birthday. This time I came to in a hospital bed. Alone. They had to use a defibrillator as well as the Narcan this time. I was told I was lucky to be alive. I felt so very far from lucky.

I made a plan to just end it all. I got my hands on a giant intermuscular needle that held fifty cc's—*way* more than enough to do the job. I spent my literal last dollar on enough junk to fill it. I went into an alley where nobody would find me until it was too late.

There I sat. Death shot in hand. I had burned just about every bridge I could. No electricity in the apartment. Eviction notice on the door. No more work because I kept calling in dead. No one knew or cared where I was or how bad I had fallen. Yet something was preventing me from going through with it. I couldn't tell you what. I called my last friend left, Tim. We made some small talk. He said he was going to watch the Sox game at a friend's house and invited me. I casually explained that I was not going to make it due to the fact that I'd be dead in an hour. Looking back, the hesitation, the calling my friend—I know now that I didn't want to die. I just didn't know what there was left to live for. I needed someone to talk me out of it. Tim did. I watched the Red Sox lose to the Yankees in game one of the 2004 playoffs. After the game, I was shocked to see my parents together for the first time since I was a kid. Tim had called my mom and told her what was going on. They told me that they had a bed for me in a rehab facility and I was leaving that night. I agreed.

At the rehab center, my only communication with the outside world were newspapers. I read about the Red Sox being down three games to none. I was depressed, but it was actually a good thing. I hadn't felt feelings in years. The therapy was intensive and lasted all day. I was eating regularly for the first time in many months. We would pile into the facility's minivan, dubbed "The Druggy Buggy" and go to twelve step meetings. I found myself laughing for the first time in what felt like an eternity. I read that the Sox had come back to beat the Yankees four games in a row in a history making performance, eventually going on to win the World Series for the first time in eighty-six years. Now I may just be a nostalgic Boston guy, but that made me feel like I could change. That I could turn my life around—and I did just that

I did ninety meetings in ninety days. It really helped me to go through the twelve steps. Step nine ended up being the most important. It's to right your wrongs. Mend relationships you tore apart with your addiction. Pay back those that hold your debt. I had my work cut out.

I had cut the roof off a box van in the Home Depot parking lot just to sell the aluminum for scrap. $3,000 in damage for a $40 fix. I went to the office of the contractor whose truck I'd damaged to admit what I had done years earlier and pay him back. His jaw nearly hit the floor.

"THAT WAS YOU!!!?? Holy SHIT!! You didn't even steal anything out of the van!" I told him I did it for scrap aluminum, and all he could do was laugh. We agreed that I would pay him $200 a month for three years. During that time he told me he had a son that had a problem with heroin. I offered to help in any way I could, but the son wasn't ready. Over the years, "How's your son?" was a common part of our monthly small talk. One December I entered his office, and there was a distinct feeling in the room. It was all over the man's face. "He's gone," he said softly, still looking down. I felt so bad for the guy and could do nothing but shake his hand. Walking out of that office, for some reason, was the first time I put it together that I was lucky to be alive—even, dare I say, grateful.

I had never found my "why" in all those therapy sessions in rehab. I still had no idea what my purpose for being alive was. I just knew I was lucky to have come out of it.

I continued to do the right things as far as working, paying bills, and not doing drugs, but there was something missing. I was going through the motions. I wondered if this was all there was. I was joyless. The only things that made me feel alive were playing music, training in mixed martial arts, or the occasional hit of dopamine when I'd date someone new. All my romantic relationships had great starts and then turned into some combination of boredom, emptiness, deception, jealousy, emotional abuse, and a host of other very unhealthy traits. I know now that my relationships failed because I had little self-respect and zero self-love. You can't freely give and receive love to and from anyone without loving yourself. You will attract the right person for you only when your life is moving toward something. I was moving nowhere.

But like compound interest, the "right things" piled up. I started, because of my martial arts, to read and learn about the human body, nutrition, exercise, supplements, and other related subjects. Without realizing it, I started to set goals and move towards them. They were all related to sport performance at first.

Then, as my interest in nonfiction continued, I became a voracious learner of any and all subjects of interest. I stumbled upon *The Success Principles* by Jack Canfield. Game over. I've been on a deep dive in personal development ever since.

During my quest for self-improvement of mind, body and spirit, I developed self-worth, self-respect, and most importantly self-love. I was happy. Chipping away at new goals all the time. I was busy focusing on me and my life's path, and as it often is, when you're not looking for it, something great falls into your lap. For me that something great was my friend, Tim, (again coming through) introducing me to my wife, Leah. Had he done so even a year earlier, it wouldn't have worked. I wouldn't have been ready for her.

Flash forward to today, and you see a life so far removed from the guy in alley about to throw it all away. Leah and I have a wonderful relationship that we work hard for, a beautiful home, investment properties, nice vehicles, great careers, annual vacations, close family bonds, and two healthy, beautiful children.

I tell you all this not to be boastful in any way at all. It's important to know that anyone can change their situation. Anyone. If the homeless, suicidal drug addict can become a functioning member of society who deeply cares about others, then any person can achieve just about any life they could imagine.

I have my why now. It took bringing people that I love on the deepest level possible into this world for me to want to make it a better place. My kids have taught me many things. Among the most important are patience and the fact that each person has an effect on the world around them.

I want what I have for everyone. Not just the house or vacations and things like that. I want everyone to be able to love deeply. To feel vibrant health, energy, and vitality. To have a sense of true, bigger than yourself purpose. To have all that they desire from this wonderful existence. It will make your life, the lives of those you love, your community, and the world just that much better.

Now, let's make it happen.

2

TAKING RESPONSIBILITY

All the various paths to a successful, meaningful, and healthy life have their start at taking responsibility. Full responsibility. For every outcome so far. The good, the bad, all of it. Your life to this point is a culmination of your subconscious programming, the thoughts you've had the most, and the actions you've taken. Taking full responsibility for where you are now in your life will be the first step in achieving the life you desire in the future. The first of many steps for putting your best self forward.

I know there are people that have terrible and unfortunate situations thrust upon them. That's real. It happens to us all. Some have tougher breaks than others. What's important, what we must take full responsibility for, is how we respond to these things. A victim is powerless. A victim that stays blaming others stays powerless. A victim who learns, grows, recovers, takes responsibility for what happens now, and makes changes is powerful. Be powerful. Be purposeful. Forgive.

The forgiveness is for you. Not anyone else. The person you're forgiving may not even deserve it. Do it anyway. Resentment, bitterness, hatred, fear, anger, and all the other negative emotions that come along with holding a grudge will keep you from your best self. They will weigh you down. They will affect decisions you make and relationships you carry on. Trust me on this one. Hold no grudges and forgive completely. That doesn't mean forget, but let go of the negative emotions you've been carrying around.

Taking responsibility means instant control and power over your life. If you blame others for what's wrong, you stay small. Your boss, your spouse, your kids, the government, that mean guy in line at CVS—remember the saying, "It's a poor carpenter that blames his tools."

There are countless things that could be an excuse for why you haven't reached the level you want. Guess what. It's your fault, and that's ok. You have the rest of your life to right the ship. The sooner you take full responsibility, the sooner you can get into the meat of it—the real reason things haven't gone your way.

Taking responsibility means taking criticism, constructive or otherwise, learning from it, and improving. Sometimes an enemy with mean-spirited criticism can point out where you could improve—something that people who love you would overlook or not have the heart to bring to your attention. You can learn from all criticism. Take responsibility and do it.

Taking responsibility means being proactive. It means that you're going to focus on what's in your control and create outcomes there. Things you have no control over won't be excuses for not getting your result. They are merely obstacles on the way to that result. The proactive person plans for what may go wrong. When it does, they are ready for it, or at least able to redirect. There will be traffic, taxes, setbacks, rain, deaths, unfair people, and scores of other things you'll have no control over. A proactive person who takes full responsibility will reach their end regardless of them. They will change course and focus on what they can control until they have it. Be that person.

When you blame people or circumstances for the state of your life, it creates a negative feedback loop. You are saying to yourself: "I'm a victim; I am powerless," and what you say to yourself is incredibly powerful, as we will discuss more in the next section. Your subconscious mind picks up self-talk, accepts it as fact, and governs the way you think and act accordingly. That powerless, victim communication to yourself gives way to a host of negative emotions like fear, anxiety, stress, and anger. These emotions are detrimental to you in so many ways. They will take a toll on relationships, productivity, sleep, self-esteem, your health, and more.

On the other hand, when you take full responsibility, it creates an upward spiral of positive thoughts and subsequent actions. All the earlier mentioned negative emotions depend on having someone or something to blame for your problems. Taking full responsibility stops those negative emotions in their tracks and gives you the power to make necessary change. It builds self-esteem and confidence. It makes you a better friend, husband or wife, parent, or business partner. It will improve every aspect of your life from job performance to your self-care regime to how you deal with someone doing forty-nine miles per hour in the passing lane. It's a game changer. Unfortunately, it's also a pretty rare quality in people. Distinguish yourself as a high functioning, productive member of society who can take control of any situation life throws at you. As Brian Tracy says, repeat the mantra, "I am responsible" several times when a problem presents itself. This instantly puts you on the offensive. It puts you in solution mode as opposed to blaming or complaining. You'll be cooler under pressure and more decisive in corrective action.

This is a 100% crucial trait for any person of high value—anyone who will achieve what they set out to accomplish in life. Make it a habit. Ingrain it into your personality. Always take full responsibility for your life, and you will be well on your way to creating the circumstances, the very existence you dream of. The life you *deserve*. It's all yours for the taking. Notice the expression, "yours for the taking." It's not yours for the receiving. You must take responsibility. Take action. Take what's yours!

3

WORD BECOMES FLESH

This is where you really need to self-evaluate. Start to audit the things you say to yourself and others. Most people don't even realize how often they limit their lives with negative self-talk or ANT's (automatic negative thoughts). Things as simple as, "I'm always late" or "I'm bad with names." Or any of the other diminishing, limiting language we use. When you say these types of things to people, you're also saying them to yourself—to your subconscious mind.

This part of your brain is incredibly powerful. When it hears these limiting phrases or thoughts, it automatically accepts them as fact. If you say you are bad with names, good luck ever actually remembering one. You've conditioned yourself to believe something and therefore act out that behavior.

Use the power of the mind for your benefit. Always. Try and clean up the limiting language. Instead of saying, "I'm bad with names," say, "I'm working on being better at remembering names." Then, guess what—you'll open a pathway for being better! You'll find that you'll start to try harder to remember names because you're "working on it." As a result, you'll remember some. Change the language, change the behavior. It's that simple. No more ANT's. No more limiting talk. Use a positive frame for all of your thoughts and phrases that pertain to you. Always say what you'd like the outcome to be.

"I get nervous meeting new people" becomes, "I want to make a good impression on people I meet." You'll end up being less nervous and more focused on being ingratiating, kind, and personable.

"I'm always late" becomes, "I'm working on leaving earlier for important meetings."

"I can't speak to an audience" becomes, "It's exhilarating to speak in public."

"I'll never get that job" becomes, "I'll improve myself to the point where I'd be an asset to any employer."

"I'm terrible with money" becomes, "I'm working on being better with my hard-earned money."

Any negative or limiting self-talk needs to be reframed. It's absolutely vital. Use the untapped power of the subconscious mind to your benefit. Take full control of your thoughts and words. You'll notice almost right away that things are changing.

You can use this reframing for thoughts and words that aren't directly about you as well. "This traffic sucks" becomes, "I have an opportunity to listen to my favorite podcast."

"I hate my job" becomes, "My job pays for my life right now and keeps food on the table while I work to find something that better suits me." When you reframe the negative things in your life, you take away their power over you. You reduce stress. You open a pathway for improvement. Remember you have complete control over your thoughts about and responses to these situations. This is what separates us from all other species: our ability to pause, use rational thinking, and direct our thoughts before we react to something. Put this into practice and see amazing results.

The title of the section is, "Word Becomes Flesh." It's just a bit catchier than "Thoughts Become Reality," which could also have been this section's title. It is a profound truth. What you spend most of your time thinking about will inevitably shape your life.

From Jesus Christ to Mark Twain, Marcus Aurelius to Ralph Waldo Emerson, Lao Tzu to Tony Robbins—scores of great men and women of philosophy from countless backgrounds, cultures, and different times in history have all come up with the same idea: that you become what you think about. That the thoughts you have will attract certain outcomes. These thoughts will shape how you view the world and how it sees you. How you talk and act. The people you attract or repel. They will govern decisions you make. What you make of a circumstance. Is it a disaster or a chance to learn, stretch, and improve your problem solving? Your thoughts will inevitably shape the quality and direction of your life.

There is so much great work on this subject. The best I can recommend is listening to Earl Nightingale's "Strangest Secret." It's thirty minutes long. Listen to it on YouTube while you go for a walk. It's perfectly put, succinct, and will expand your knowledge and understanding of this subject better than I ever could.

For now, let's start by being aware of all the thoughts you have during the day. Any thought that will take you away from your goals or that doesn't serve you in a positive way needs to be examined. Why am I thinking this? How can I reframe this thought to serve me better?

For example, let's say you have a goal to make more money and spend less. If in your spare time your thoughts cause you to want to shop online, ask, "Do I need this? Will this help me make more money?" If it's a training, certification, or book you could learn from, then maybe the answer is yes. Most likely the answer would be no. Reframe. How can I better spend this time to concentrate on making more money? The Google search will switch from shoes to education. Once you are conscious of these thought patterns that brought the phone to your face and caused you to start shopping, you're on your way to taking control and shaping your life. If a thought doesn't serve you or help you reach your goals, reframe it or cut it out completely.

It starts with consciously directing your thoughts. Then the actions fall into congruence with the directed thoughts. A day of directed, goal oriented thoughts and actions is powerful. You can get a lot done or at least started. String together days like that and you'll have a life changing month. String those together and you've done the "impossible" in a year.

The most important things to think about ALL the time are your goals. If your mind is consistently on your goals, there is no way you won't move toward them. The next section will teach you how to set them.

For now, just remember you become what you think about. You become what you say. Clean up all negativity in thoughts and speech. Spend time picturing yourself in your dream situations. Work, relationship, social life, vacations, your ideal body—all of it. Say you are on your way to those things. Out loud. Your subconscious mind will start pushing up thoughts that will cause actions to make it so. If you say, "I'm on my way to losing twenty pounds" and later a thought arises to get Uber Eats to deliver a pizza and brownies, *believe* me, there will be a feeling of incongruence. That is the moment to reframe. The incongruity is your old patterns and new goals colliding. The thought, "I'm on my way to losing twenty pounds. The picture you hold in your mind of how you'd look in that swimsuit and how you'd feel twenty pounds lighter is colliding with an old pattern that doesn't serve you. You will then have a chance at a new action. Perhaps a trip to the market to buy ingredients for a delicious healthy meal. Victory! The goal is as good as yours if you direct your thoughts and take action!

It's one of the only things we have complete control over in this life. What we think. How we react. You can't control what happens all the time. You can control how you react every time. That's powerful. Harness that power when undesirable circumstances arise. Control your reactions. Focus your thoughts on solutions and take action. You can diminish all negative circumstances this way. You'll be a more effective person in every area of your life when you have full dominion over your thoughts and speech.

4

HAVE A TARGET

An archer steps out onto the range. Sun on his shoulders, gentle breeze at his back. He takes an arrow from his quill and knocks it. He draws and anchors the bow. Takes aim…shit, wait— there's no target.

How absurd would it be to load up all the archery gear and head over to a range with no targets? Yet that's exactly what most of us are doing. We have poor goals if we have any at all.

Goals are the most important part of any success strategy. Physical, emotional, spiritual, financial, educational, business, romantic, or personal success all comes from skillfully setting goals. Goals are starting with the end in mind. Like a ship's captain with a clear course, a good goal will guide your every step.

Picture a farmer whose goal was, "Oh, I don't know, maybe I'll grow some things you can eat, I guess, see how it goes." Come harvest time, I'd be willing to bet his yield would reflect that aim. You need to know exactly what you want to harvest to know exactly when to plant, what the soil amendments and necessary Ph levels are for that specific crop, how to fertilize and water, whether to plant in a shadier spot or full sun, how and when to prune for maximum yield, and the list goes on. Goals are no different. They need to be incredibly specific in order to direct the mind to that particular end.

Now imagine two people who want to improve their strength and lose weight. One's goal is, "I want to lose my belly fat and get stronger." The action plan is to eat healthy food, cut out the morning muffin, and get to the gym more often. The other's goal is, "Lose eighteen pounds by February twenty-first for my vacation to Aruba. I want to rock that red two-piece I wore four years ago when I was in the best shape of my life and feel amazing doing it. I also want to be able to perform my first pull-up and get three pull-ups before the trip. The action plan is to begin an intermittent fasting protocol with a six-hour eating window of 12-6 p.m. I will completely cut out sugar and flour until 2/21. I will eat only lean protein, healthy fats, and high quality carbs in the form of colorful vegetables and low glycemic berries. I will keep my calorie intake about 600 below maintenance level to average a pound lost per week. I have twenty weeks, so eighteen pounds should be well attainable in that time. I will weigh in every morning to track my progress and adjust calories accordingly. No cheat meals until I'm on Aruba in a Bali bed by the sea in that red two-piece. I will get 10,000 steps every day. I will do intervals two times per week. I will strength train three times per week. I will do banded pull-ups for the first month, lowering the band tension as possible. Next, I will do the negative portion of the pull-up and dead hangs every workout, adding time to the hang and reps to the negatives until I can do my first pull-up. Then I will do fifteen sets of one pull-up each workout until I can get two. Then I will do ten sets of two each workout until I can hit three.

Who will be more likely to reach their goals? Obvious, right? The two people wanted very similar things. Maybe they even had similar drive and skill sets. Better goals equal better results. The best goals are SMART goals.

Specific. Measurable. Attainable. Relevant. Time bound. SMART.

The second person's goal was incredibly Specific. She was able to Measure the progress of her goals with the morning weigh-ins and as she got more and more repetitions of pull-ups. Her goal was Attainable in that she gave herself enough time to perform a realistic feat. It was Relevant to her greater goal of lifelong fitness and longevity. It was Time bound because she had a date to get it all done by.

Setting goals this way sets you up for success. It puts everything into perspective and helps you create the perfect plan to accomplish it.

Dream big! There is almost nothing that you can imagine that you can't achieve. As the immortal Napoleon Hill, the OG of personal development, said, "Conceive, believe, and achieve." Belief is the key word of those three. You have to have faith in yourself and the plan you've created.

The way to develop that faith is to take a dream of yours and decide to make it a reality. Conceive it in your mind. Vividly imagine how you'd feel with your dream actually achieved. Say your dream is of a big, beautiful home. Picture the neighborhood, the shape and size, the color, the trees, the foot bridge over the koi pond. Involve all your senses. Hear the waterfall trickle into your infinity edge saltwater pool. Feel its mist kiss your face on a warm summer day. Hear your children shrieking with delight and splashing. Smell the fragrant flowers in the garden. Taste the frozen margarita in your hand. This will activate and utilize the power of your subconscious mind.

The faith will come as you are able to push out negative thoughts like, "I'll never afford that" and instead ask questions like, "How would I be able to afford that?" The negative thought is a command to your subconscious mind and will be accepted as fact and produce results in accordance. But the question taps into the vast storehouse of wisdom you carry around with you. The mind is powerful, and good questions will unchain that power.

You will turn on your Reticular Activating System. With out getting too technical, the Reticular Activating System (RAS) is the part of your brain that is responsible for what you pay attention to. There are thousands and thousands of things for your brain to process every second. The RAS funnels what it believes to be relevant to your attention. Start asking good questions and see what "falls into your lap."

With the question, "How can I afford that dream house?" the RAS will hone in on business or investment opportunities, classes to improve skills, free workshops, wealth building seminars, real estate videos on YouTube, opportunities to meet the right people, foreclosures in the desired neighborhood, saltwater pool company ads—unlock that power with good questions.

The final step in developing the faith necessary for big goals is chunking them down. With an accurate gauge on what it would really take to achieve a big goal and the subconscious mind and RAS working on its behalf, you'll know what steps need to be taken to get started. That's all you need. Who cares how you'll finally get there? Just start! Set small SMART goals in congruence with the big one. As you crush these little mile marker goals, your faith in your ability and the process will come pouring in. Don't forget to celebrate these wins either. Take just a moment to pat yourself on the back. If you're on your way to a goal, you're already a success.

Even if when you start you have no idea how you'll get to the end, each step, each small goal reached will teach you how to set the next one. It will be like a torch to illuminate the next bit of the darkened path. Keep at this and you'll amaze yourself with how far you can go.

Write. Goals. Down. Something powerful happens when you take pen to paper. There is a deeper connection with the brain. Use it to your advantage. Get a journal, keep it next to your bed, and write down your goals every morning as soon as you get up. Talk about priming the RAS and subconscious mind to focus on and attract the right things! Then each night, read the goals out loud. Spend a few minutes picturing them accomplished. Visualization is a powerful tool. Remember, use a vivid image involving all of your senses. If you take only one thing from this book and make it your own, a part of your everyday life, I implore you to make good goal setting that thing. This alone can and will dramatically change the trajectory of your life.

Have faith. "Ask and you shall receive. Seek and you shall find. Knock and it shall be opened to you."

5

SERVE

In the words of the great Zig Ziglar, "You can have everything in life you want, if you just help people get what they want." Mr. Ziglar was a master salesman. That quote is from his seminars for training salespeople. If you're in sales, you know how literally true that statement is. However, I've come to realize that it's also true for everyone else on this planet as well.

The highest point in life is giving. You get a dopamine hit. You feel amazing. Your heartbeat kicks up a few notches. You're in tune with the person who is the subject of your service. Whether it's generosity with time, money, advice, protection, or just a smile, it makes our world a better place. It also makes you operate within a higher vibration. That vibration will quite literally attract favorable circumstances to you. Like attracts like.

If you serve the people in your life, family, coworkers, or just people in the supermarket with kindness, generosity, and a spirit of gratitude, the world will open up to you. The ancient wisdom says it all. It's better to give than to receive. Smile at the world, and the world will smile back. It's been said countless times because it's true.

Other people are the key to all our riches and rewards in life. They are the ones who will buy your product, invest in your company, show you that one thing you're missing, choose to sell their home to you over the sixteen other buyers with similar offers, give you that promotion, come to your aid in time of need, approve you for that loan, let you merge in traffic, make the fresh pot of coffee instead of giving you the last bit of burned coffee in the old pot, give you the best deal possible, coach and mentor you, and all other good things that will come to you in life, big or small.

Have you ever met someone with a wonderful, warm smile that asked great questions or gave great advice or maybe even just held a door for you? They did something small that made you appreciate them, and their energy or vibration was attractive. It was a selfless spirit of service that drew you in. There is a great philosophy that says, "Make every person you encounter glad that they met you." If you approach every day and every encounter like this, you will have all that you could possibly desire in life. One way I remember to be this way is called a door trigger. I got this gem from Brendon Burchard, and it works wonders. Every time you cross a threshold, either entering or exiting, say to yourself, "Here enters (or embarks) a happy man ready to serve." It sets you up for success every time. Implement this, and it will change your life forever.

One of the best examples of service and its rewards I know of is from the wonderful book *Business Secrets From the Bible* by Rabbi Daniel Lapin. In it, he tells the story of a day in the life of Grandpa Lapin, a peddler.

If you don't know, a peddler was a very common livelihood from generations past—a door to door salesman and trader.

In this hypothetical day of Grandpa Lapin, he starts by knocking on the door of a woman. He asks her if she has anything she no longer has use for. She tells him that she has a table she was going to get rid of and that the city was going to charge her five dollars for its removal. Grandpa Lapin offers to buy the table from her for five dollars instead. He then makes a trip to the hardware store to buy a dollar's worth of materials to fix up the table.

His next stop is to a home where he asks if they have any need for a new table. The people do, and they were prepared to spend $20 at the furniture store for a new one. They are happy to buy the peddler's refurbished table for $10.

You see, the woman was up ten dollars by saving the five for the table removal and the purchase price of five dollars received from Grandpa Lapin. The other family was up $10 also from the money saved buying the refurbished table. The hardware store had a customer, and Grandpa Lapin made himself a slick profit of four dollars. The simple act of serving your community enriches everyone.

Although Rabbi Lapin was answering the question, "Where does money come from?" with this anecdote, I believe it's perfect for this section on serving people as well. One of the Business Secrets from the Bible is that we were created to obsessively concern ourselves with the needs of others. To serve our family and community. God's tangible reward for serving your neighbors is money! The story of Grandpa Lapin beautifully and simply illuminates this point.

You don't need to be a Jew or Christian or religious at all to understand the intrinsic value of serving others. Service to another person enriches you both emotionally, advances you with spiritual currency, and a lot of times, brings in cold hard cash.

When you get up every morning, no matter what the work you do is, you are rendering service. Pour yourself into it.

Later I will tell the story of a wellness client of mine, "John." I served him simply by planning diet and exercise programming for him and consulting with him on dietary supplements. Those small changes upward spiraled into huge changes for John. Among many other things, he vastly improved his health, all but quit drinking, improved upon his family relationships, and upgraded his performance and work. Long story short, through serving John I was able to touch the lives of his wife and children, his employer, the people that came to work under him after a promotion, his clients, his friends, and his extended family, all while helping to provide for my own family. You could say I was just doing my job, and I was. However, I chose my work because I genuinely love to help people improve their lives, and I pour my heart into it. For that I am greatly rewarded, spiritually and financially.

Live a life of service—at home, at your work, in your very essence. Make it a hallmark of yours, and you will always attract good people to you. People who will be drawn to help you. The right people at the right times. Your own existence will be improved just by the simple act of being kind, generous, and supportive to others all while improving the lives of those around you. Win-win—now go get 'em.

6

NUTRITION

For this subject, I could write several books, let alone a quick section of a small book. It's a vastly nuanced subject that can be looked at many different ways.

That said, fundamental concepts of good nutrition are not and should not be complicated. For the purposes of this book, I'll keep it very straightforward and simple.

If I could do it in just a paragraph, it'd be this. Avoid all processed and ultra processed foods like the plague. Eat only things you would find in nature—organic, no pesticides, non gmo, grass fed, grass finished, no hormones or antibiotics, wild caught, pasture raised, natural food. Eating healthy plants and animals makes you a healthy animal. Prioritize protein and colorful vegetables. Have at least twelve hours of the day when you're not eating. Eat only at meal time, no snacks in between. Your digestion is most powerful around midday, so eat your bigger meal at lunch. Walk for five to fifteen minutes after each meal. That's it in a nutshell. If you followed that to the letter, you'd be a healthy person. Fact.

It can go much deeper, though, so let's dip our toes in a bit more without getting too complicated. Let's start with the one thing you should completely avoid at all costs: hydrogenated vegetable and seed oils! Vegetable and seed oils were invented as industrial products for automobiles and other machinery and somehow made it into our food supply. Further changing their structure by adding hydrogen for shelf life is turning something bad for you into something deadly. They are easily oxidized and cause inflammation, weight gain and heart disease. Don't use them or eat things that contain them, ever.

Then there are the two that should be far and few between: sugar and grain. I love sweets and breads and pasta and rice and bread…and did I mention bread? Grains and sugar are friggin' delicious. I know. I get it.

I would recommend a 90%/10% split for these two. 90% of the time, get your carbs from green leafy or cruciferous vegetables and all the other vastly colorful vegetables and fruits (mostly berries—they are low glycemic and high in antioxidants). Get your starches from root vegetables like sweet potatoes or Japanese yams. The other 10% of the time, have a pizza, have a cookie, have whatever you please. Live life. Don't deprive yourself. Don't be antisocial and avoid dinners out. Live a full life that includes an ice cream sundae…10% of the time!

Speaking of pizza and ice cream, I have a very helpful and important tip. On that 10% cheat meal, flex meal, diet break, or however you'd like to refer to it, make sure it's planned. Schedule it in advance. If you know you're going out for dinner with friends, let it be then. They will marvel at slender, healthy you eating cheesecake. If there's a busy day this week in your schedule and you know you may have to stop for something less than perfectly healthy, make it the flex meal. Just know when it will be and plan ahead by having one tablespoon of apple cider vinegar mixed with eight ounces of room temperature water ready. Drink that down twenty to thirty minutes before your flex meal. It will help with blood sugar levels and subsequent insulin response. That's a big one. Do it every time you go rogue, and it will be a serious ace up your sleeve.

One more flex meal must. Never have two flex meals in a row. The reason is that most (let's face it, all) cheat meals are going to involve grains, starches, and/or sugar—as they damn well should! This will fill up your glycogen stores in the liver and muscles. That in and of itself is fine. We use the glycogen stores to regulate blood sugar while fasting or during intense exercise. However, when the stores are full and you eat another flex meal with too many unhealthy carbs, there will be no place for the glucose you don't burn up as fuel to go other than fat storage. So make sure there are several healthy, lower carb meals and preferably a workout in between flex meals to make sure that the glucose you consume will either be used or have room to be stored in your liver and muscles as glycogen.

Next, the world's greatest breakfast. I recommend this to every single one of my health coaching clients. It's not groundbreaking or secret. Nope, it's just the humble smoothie. But it's a very particular set of ingredients at the perfect ratio. You see, hundreds of different cultures around the world have been eating soup for breakfast for the last couple thousand years. It's easy to digest and hydrating. Simple. Ayurvedic wisdom tells us digestion is at its strongest midday. So it makes sense to have an easy to digest meal first thing. It saves all that energy usually used for digestion to be used to power you through your morning. So we take that ancient wisdom and improve upon it with this recipe.

1 cup of whole milk and/or
16 oz. of spring water
1 cup organic blueberries or blackberries
¼ an avocado (½ for higher caloric needs)
2 cups of organic spinach
1 scoop of your favorite protein powder

You have low glycemic carbs packed full of antioxidants and phytonutrients, lean protein, and healthy fat. It's delicious, incredibly healthy, easy to digest, and it's actually filling. Take your time drinking it, though—thirty to sixty minutes.

A quick word on diets. While there are good elements to them all, we should be looking for a healthy lifestyle as opposed to a diet. The only exception is if you're on a vegan diet for ethical reasons. If that's the case, you're a noble person. I love you and what you're doing. That said, if it's for health reasons, I believe there are a few holes. There are too many things missing for long term optimal health—mostly fat soluble vitamins, iron that's perfectly bio available, and protein. Yes, you can supplement for those things. However, I believe it's better for one's health and wellness to get them from high quality food. The polar opposite of a vegan diet would be the carnivore diet. In my opinion there are many holes there as well. Most importantly, we need to eat plants. They are full of antioxidants and phytonutrients you can't get anywhere else. Period.

Keto, Atkins, Mediterranean, Paleo, South Beach, and any other diet can "work," and there's great things about all of them. Sure, if you normally eat muffins and mocha lattes for breakfast, a sandwich with fries and soda for lunch, and take out, beer, and Ben and Jerry's for dinner before your nighttime snack of nachos, then any of those diets would be drastically healthier and would help you get closer to a healthy weight.

We shouldn't aim to diet. We should make eating whole, healthy and unprocessed foods 90% of the time a lifestyle. That's really it. But if a certain diet works for you, then of course, use it. I don't care what camp you're in. I just want the healthiest and happiest you possible. If only meat or no animal products or any diet in between makes you happy and healthy, I'm all in for you.

Supplements are necessary for most people to round off nutrition. Even a near perfect diet will have some supplementary needs for optimal health. The best way to know exactly what you are deficient in is functional medicine lab testing. Find a practitioner like me who offers at home lab testing. However, there are a few suggestions for pretty much anyone that I'll make here.

If you're not eating fatty fish like mackerel, salmon, or sardines four times a week, you are undoubtedly out of balance with your omega-6 and omega-3 ratio. Find an organic omega-3 supplement that's high in EPA.

If you live in an area that has a winter season, then you definitely need to be taking vitamin D during the months when you're not outside getting naturally occurring vitamin D from the sun. Vitamin D levels affect your immune system, energy levels, bones, skin, and much more.

If you're not eating seven to nine servings of vegetables each day, I would strongly recommend a greens powder or pill. Try and get the seven to nine servings in your diet. If you did and took the supplement as well, there would be no harm in it. You can't have too many cancer-fighting immune boosting antioxidants.

65% of people are magnesium deficient. It's the main micronutrient responsible for turning on your parasympathetic nervous system (PNS) and relaxing. Staying out of stress, turning on the PNS, and keeping all the subsequent stress hormones out of your bloodstream is one of the most important things you can do for overall health and wellbeing. It will be important whether your goals are weight loss, muscle building, reproduction, longevity, or restorative sleep. There is a 65% chance you need more magnesium and no harm if you supplement and have extra.

I would recommend a methylated multivitamin every day for every person on the planet. It's a great idea just to cover all the bases and round out a healthy diet. Make sure it's high quality and activated or methylated.

Nutrition should be something that takes precedence. It costs a few more dollars to get all the organic, no pesticides, non-gmo, grass fed, grass finished, no hormones or antibiotics, wild caught, pasture raised, natural food. But this is your health, energy, longevity, immune system, and how you feel every day we're talking about. You are worth every extra penny it costs to eat and supplement for optimal health.

Get inspired! Look up healthy recipes and have fun with your nutrition (and cheat meals)!

7

FASTING

Fasting is the one of the most powerful weapons in your health and wellness arsenal, and it's completely free. Actually it saves you time and money—less food cost and less time cooking and cleaning.

Fasting has many, many benefits. Things like rebalancing hormones, improving immune function, autophagy (more on that later), calorie restriction for those of us looking to lose weight, mental clarity, improved gut health, increased human growth hormone, and more. You'll go into a ketogenic state after glycogen stores are depleted, you'll get energy from stored fat, and it gives your digestive system a break. Digesting food is a ton of work for the body. When you fast, your body can concentrate on cellular repair and the immune system, which is mostly in your gut. It's an amazing tool to improve your health.

You may think there is no way that you could ever go sixteen, twenty-four, or forty-eight hours without food, let alone a seven-day or beyond water fast. Unless you're hypoglycemic and are constantly in a catabolic state struggling to maintain a healthy weight, you can.

Our hunter gatherer ancestors would have never survived to pass on their genes if we couldn't. There were unsuccessful hunts. There were times of the year when there was nothing to gather. We undoubtedly evolved fasting. Our endocrine system tells the tale. We have four hormones that raise blood sugar to keep it at a healthy level when no food is available. They are cortisol, human growth hormone, glucagon, and adrenaline. That's right, we have four different ways for our body to keep a healthy blood sugar when no glucose is available in the diet. Why would that be, other than to help us through lean times? The human body is brilliant.

So not only is fasting possible, in my opinion, it's necessary. There are too many health benefits to not incorporate it into your health and wellness plan. Put it this way: if the pharmaceutical industry could someday incapsulate and sell a drug with the benefits of fasting, it would be the most popular drug on the planet. And you would buy it. But it's here for you now and for free.

Longer fasts induce a state called autophagy. It literally means to self-eat. It sounds scary, but it's actually a very good thing for you. This is when you clean house on a cellular level. Your body will find bacteria and old, redundant, or bad cells like cancer cells and break them down to be used as fuel—again showing how brilliant the human body is. A lot of people worry about going catabolic and using muscle for gluconeogenesis (creating sugar) during autophagy. It will not happen. Muscle sparing Human Growth Hormone (HGH) can raise up to 1000% higher levels to preserve muscle tissue while fasting. Hence our amazing body will only utilize the unnecessary, decaying, or dangerous cells.

Then when you refeed or break fast, especially with something high in phosphorus like bone broth, your stem cells will replace the self-eaten cells with brand new ones. So you are aging in reverse at a cellular level when you enter autophagy. More on breaking fast for optimal health later.

There are many ways to fast. What follows are the simplest and most effective fasting protocols. Again, keep in mind that fasting should not be done by people who are hypoglycemic, catabolic, or who struggle to keep weight on. But everyone else will benefit from these protocols with weight loss and all the other wonderful effects that come with fasting.

1. Intermittent fasting. This is the easiest way to dip your toes into the fasting game. Start with an eight-hour eating window. The best window is 7 a.m. - 3 p.m. This is in line with our circadian rhythm and gives a ton of time to digest before bed. However, for most people's schedule 12 p.m. – 8 p.m. works best. You can have three meals in that eight-hour window. Using the 12 p.m. – 8 p.m. feeding window as an example, then make the meals at 12 p.m., 4 p.m. and 8 p.m., giving you four hours in between each meal. You can do two meals in that same feeding window as well. As you get better at fasting and you become fat adapted, which means you're more able to use stored fat as fuel in the form of ketones, you can shrink your feeding window. Try a six-hour window, then four. A three or four-hour feeding window is as small as you can go while still having two meals. After that you can get down to the OMAD protocol, the big

daddy of intermittent fasting. That's One Meal A Day, which is about a twenty-four-hour fast each day.

2. Once a week OMAD. For this you would use any intermittent fasting window or the standard minimum fasting every human should do of twelve hours, but once a week you'd have a twenty-four-hour fast. For example, you'd have dinner at 5 p.m. Sunday and fast until dinner at 5 p.m. Monday. Then resume whichever protocol you've been using on Tuesday.

3. Once a week forty-eight-hour fast. This will be the same as the above, but just add another twenty-four hours of fasting, i.e. from Sunday 5 p.m. until Tuesday 5 p.m. Here's where major benefits kick in. Not only tremendous fat burning, but also autophagy sets in somewhere in that fasting window.

4. Monthly or quarterly seventy-two-hour fasts. Detox, cleanse, and renew cells.

5. Quarterly or annual week-long and beyond fasts. A great way to jumpstart a new eating protocol. Great time for a de-load week in the gym. (Fancy fitness talk for a week off, which you would do every three to six months)

It may sound like WAY too much to handle. Or like it'd be dangerous. It's not either of those things. You can do it.

75% of Americans are overweight; 60% are clinically obese. This means that the average person could go thirty to fifty days without food. Now I'm not recommending that anyone do that at all, especially without a doctor's supervision. But it's possible. This is why the human body is so very good at storing fat. We evolved to be able to use those stores when we struck out on hunts and could gather nothing to eat, and *that* is why 75% of the population is overweight. It's our brilliant, fat storing body colliding with this modern era of desk jobs and Uber Eats. We are not moving nearly as much as our ancestors. We have a near endless supply of calories, most of which are products, not even food at all.

If we live a bit closer to the way our early ancestors did, we can use these bodies of ours the way they were intended. All that means is move more (we'll get way into that in the next section), eat natural food, and fast sometimes. Easy peasy.

Finally, make sure you break fast properly. In a perfect world, you would break a longer fast (forty-eight hours or more) with bone broth. Give that an hour to enter your system and then eat healthy, natural food in a modest proportion for your first meal back. Don't have a cheat meal straight away and don't binge. That's it. For intermittent fasting, have a protein and healthy fat centric meal first to keep the blood sugar spike down. Just don't start with sugar or high glycemic carbs.

If you can train yourself to use fasting in any of the above protocols in any combination that works for your life and schedule, you will *drastically* improve your health and well-being. Make it part of your life and see truly amazing results!

8

MOVE. YOUR. BODY!

Muscles, tendons, cartilage, ligaments, strong bones, and intricately articulating joints all masterfully designed for dynamic movement, and what do we do with it all? We sit at a table and eat cornflakes. Then we sit in a car. Then we sit at a desk. Then we sit in the car again before sitting on a couch, all before lying in a bed. I wish this was an exaggeration, but for a great deal of the western world it sadly is not.

The subject of exercise and human movement, like nutrition, is an incredibly complex one. A million and one experts are giving conflicting advice, fad exercise programs, gadgets, classes, and many, many other things combining to make it an Everest of information and almost impossible to start.

Let's keep it simple. Let's go with fundamentally sound, tried and true information. Here's everything you need to know to be healthy and to use this amazing body we've been given properly.

Your movement every week should include 10,000+ steps a day, resistance training, stretching and joint mobility, low and slow (zone two) cardio, functional strength training for balance and proper movement, and super high intensity intervals to increase your Vo2 max. If you can create a weekly routine that incorporates all those aspects, you will be extremely physically fit and healthy. Your bones, muscles, tendons, and heart will last a lot longer than without, bolstering your longevity and the quality of life you bring to those years.

Here I will give you a super brief explanation of all those components. 10,000 steps is about five miles. Do you need to go for a five-mile walk every day? Not at all. I would recommend getting a step tracker. See how many steps you've put in each day around dinner time. You may be surprised what errands and playing with the kids will give you for a step count. If you have 6,500 steps at dinner, go out for a walk after dinner and put in the other 3,500 steps.

Resistance training can be done with free weights, nautilus machines, resistance bands, your own body weight, or any combination of those. You want to keep it easy if you're a beginner. Develop tendon strength and lifting technique first. As you progress, you'll want to bring sets close to muscular failure. This is when your muscles are so fatigued you can't perform one more clean rep. This allows you the most time under mechanical tension possible for that set. This is where the magic of hypertrophy (muscle building) kicks in to its fullest. Because your brain believes everything you do physically during the day is for your very survival, your central nervous system will signal for more muscle growth when you take an exercise to muscle failure. The brain will perceive this exertion as a threat to your survival and adapt with muscle growth accordingly.

Your stretching can be done before or after any workout. There are yoga classes and straight-up stretch classes. My best advice is to get warm first. Your body will respond better to the stretching stimulus after your core is warmed up. I prefer a mix of dynamic stretching and static stretching with an emphasis on the dynamic. Also, things like yoga or performing a horse stance that combine muscle and tendon stretching, joint mobility, and strength are amazing. Try and remember to move all your joints through their full range of motion a couple times a week. The hinge on a door that is constantly opened will never rust.

Zone two cardio is low and slow, like an easy pace on the elliptical, bike, or rowing machine. Or something like a brisk walk. Anything that elevates your heart rate but is sustainable for twenty to forty minutes. If you can have a conversation that is not super labored, you're in the sweet spot. Zone two is great for your circulation and cardiovascular health.

Functional strength will mean slightly different things to different people. If you're seventy-five years old, it should be slow squats in and out of a chair, getting up off of the floor using only one hand, standing on one leg, trying it with your eyes closed, step ups, weighted carries and dead hangs from a pull-up bar. All these things will assist in everyday life and can and should be done by people of any age. Older people *must* do them to maintain a quality of life. If you're an athlete or you do physical work, you should train with sport or labor specific movements and stretches. Every human should work on grip strength, balancing and moving on one leg, stepping up, carrying, and all other functional movements.

Hight Intensity Interval Training (or HIIT) is doing a super intense movement for a duration and then resting for a duration. Example, a one minute sprint on the assault bike, then a thirty second rest. Repeat for ten cycles. You can sprint on a treadmill or track, you can do burpees, tuck jumps, full bore jump rope, hill runs, stadium stairs, or any intense exercises you can only do in short bursts. You can play with your working and resting times. Find what's just right for you. This type of workout will improve cardiovascular health and endurance, burn a ton of calories during and after the workout and increase your Vo2 max. Vo2 Max is one of the biggest markers for longevity out there along with grip strength.

In practice, this would look like:

Monday: total body resistance training with heavier weights and low to mid reps focused on compound lifts. Thirty minutes low and slow zone two cardio post lifting.

Tuesday: yoga, tai chi or Qu gong class for active recovery and stretching.

Wednesday: total body resistance training with higher reps and lighter weights focused on single joint exercises. Fifteen minutes of HIIT post lifting.

Thursday: rest day. Sauna, steam room, massage, ice bath, stretching, or meditation. Or all of them! Just get the 10,000+ steps in.

Friday: functional training. Deep body weight squats (full range of motion), 18" step ups preformed slowly, Turkish get ups with kettlebell, timed dead hangs, farmer's carry (both hands carrying a weight), suitcase carry (one hand carrying a weight), and practice balancing on one leg with your eyes closed. Thirty minutes of low and slow zone 2 cardio.

Saturday: total body resistance training. Focus on muscle groups you need the improvement in and or muscles that you find recover well. Fifteen minutes of HIIT.

Sunday: fun cardio. Pickup basketball, spin class, yard work, or any physical activity that makes you sweat and gets your heart rate elevated.

I know this is a lot. This is what exercise would look like in a perfect world without time restraints and with unlimited money for gym memberships and classes and hour-long massages. Just do something, within your time availability and financial comfort, that's as close to the above "perfect" week as possible. Remember, pushups, pull-ups, sit-ups, burpees, jumping jacks, side bends, toe touches, running, walking, fresh air, sunshine, hot and cold showers (instead of steam room and ice bath), stretching, yoga, tai chi or qi gong instruction on YouTube, shadow boxing, and much more are free. You can make the time for important things. Your lifespan, health span (the quality of your later years) and how you feel and look right now are pretty frickin' important. You deserve to feel amazing.

For the super time restricted person, I have developed a ten-minute routine to be done first thing in the morning. Set your alarm clock for ten minutes earlier. Done. No excuses. Ten dynamic movements, each for one minute. Combine this with 10,000+ steps per day, and you're well on your way to living a fit and healthy life.

1. Pushups.
2. Squats.
3. Hip thrusts.
4. Plank.
5. Tuck jumps.
6. Pull-ups.

7. Split lunges.
8. Leg lifts.
9. Handstand.
10. High knees.

In ten minutes you have stimulated every major muscle group, kicked up endorphins, articulated many joints through a healthy range of motion, gotten your heart rate up, and improved circulation. Not a bad start to the day.

I promise: if you make this a daily ritual, you will be a stronger, healthier person. As you improve in strength and conditioning, you will inevitably be adding reps to each exercise. Move on to a higher level of difficulty for the exercises when you can. Increase range of motion and rep speed. This way the workout will always be a challenge. Feel free to double up on a movement or add a new movement and make it an eleven-minute routine. Add movements and time to the routine as needed. This constant progression will keep you consistently improving in your strength and conditioning.

I find that exercise is the low hanging fruit in health and wellness. It's a great place to start, and it will inevitably improve other aspects of your life by acting as a ball carrier habit. A ball carrier habit is one thing you add to your life that, like a running back on a football team, can move the whole team forward to a new line of scrimmage.

My best example of this is the earlier mentioned client of mine we'll call John. John drank too much, his diet was atrocious, he was way overweight, he felt tired all the time, his body ached constantly, his marriage was in trouble, he and his wife argued often about money, he had regrets about not spending enough time with his kids, he was in jeopardy of losing his job due to poor performance and showing up late and hung over, he was always stressed, and he had high blood pressure. At his last doctor's visit before meeting with me, he was told he was pre-diabetic.

I told John that his current lifestyle was killing him. He agreed. I started him with a simple 10,000 steps per day. He got a step counter and went for an evening walk with his wife and kids after dinner to hit the 10,000.

He did this for a month and said he felt better just because he was doing *something*.

We added ten minutes of body weight resistance training every other day, and something clicked. John had been an athlete in his youth, and he took very well to the resistance training. He felt "Sore in a good way" for the first time in years. He saw some pretty quick results in the form of a weight drop for the first time since he'd been married and a little shoulder muscle popping out. That was it. He was hooked.

We increased the workouts to include cardio and stretching. He asked about a diet to go along with and help maximize the workouts. I put him on a lower carb, no sugar, no grain diet with intermittent fasting. The weight dropped even more.

Being hung over diminished his performance in the workouts, and as a result his drinking started to take a back seat during the week.

On and on we went, tweaking diet and exercise routines to meet his new goals.

John currently is at his college weight and is in the best shape of his life in how he looks *and* feels. He's off blood pressure medication. His pre-diabetic status has been reversed. He drinks only on special occasions and celebrations with friends and family. As a result of not going to the bar every day after work, he has saved a ton of money and been more available for his wife and kids. He's improved his job performance so much he's received a promotion. He feels and looks younger. He's sleeping better. His stress is under control. All the big problems John had when we started are diminished. The quality of his life and the lives of those who love him have improved drastically.

His wife told me that everything started to change when he said, "I'm trying not to be so fat and cranky. You want to go for a walk with me?" Now that's what I call an upward spiral! To start with getting your steps in and end up with a promotion at work, drastically improved family life, more financial security, and a clean bill of health.

The benefits of exercise are tremendous. It's the most profound tool in your health and wellness toolbox. With proper daily movement, you will:

- Have more energy
- Sleep better at night
- Increase bone density and strength
- Experience a more positive mood due to serotonin production while combating mental dysphoria like depression, anxiety, and stress
- Promote a healthy weight
- See a drastic reduction in all-cause mortality rate by increasing things like Vo2 max and grip strength
- Improve blood sugar levels and insulin resistance
- Enhance cardiovascular and cardio respiratory health

- Increase lifespan and, more importantly, health span
- Bolster the immune system
- Reduce joint and muscle pain
- Increase strength
- Reduce high blood pressure
- Boost confidence
- Improve cognitive function and brain health
- Improve digestion and metabolic functions
- Improves endocrine system function
- Promotes toxin removal (by sweating), which will boost liver function.

Again, if the pharmaceutical industry could encapsulate these benefits and sell them to us in a pill, we'd all line up for it. However, fortunately for us, all this is free and available today with only positive side effects.

Make intelligent daily movement a part of your life. Do it for yourself and for those who love you. You are worth the effort.

9

MEDITATION

If you're like I used to be, when you think of meditation, you picture a Buddhist monk in a flowing orange robe seated cross-legged on a Tibetan mountainside or a Kung Fu master in a horse stance, eyes shut, doing heavy breathing exercises under a waterfall or some other far-off and grandiose epic scene.

The above examples, however super cool they may be, are not the only situations where meditation is necessary, beneficial, or practiced. It can be done by anyone almost anywhere. It doesn't need to take hours, there's no need for a vow of silence, and as a matter of fact you don't even have to be good at it to start or get some benefit from the practice.

Admittedly, I was late to the mediation party. I thought it was some esoteric, unnecessary thing that only monks, eastern martial arts practitioners, and hippies did. I thought the juice wasn't worth the squeeze. What could I really get from sitting with my eyes closed quietly? I could be learning something, doing something.

I know now that when you meditate you most certainly are doing something, and you undoubtedly are learning very valuable things as well.

Now that it's part of my everyday routine and I'm getting better at it, the rewards are compounding. It can and will do the same for you if you put in the effort.

Meditation, when practiced daily, will be the key to your positive change. It will aid and accelerate all your goals and a healthy lifestyle.

The benefits of meditation include:

- Improves cognitive functions like better memory and recall
- Lowers stress and improves stress response
- Lowers anxiety
- Improves sleep

- Enhances your abilities for kindness and empathy
- Promotes self-awareness
- Increases your attention span
- Bolsters self-confidence
- Lowers informatory response
- Helps break addictions
- Lowers pain
- Decreases blood pressure

That list of mental and physical benefits should tell the story. Simple, quick, and zero cost. Set aside just a few minutes of your day and make it a habit. Trust me, it's powerful.

Everything we do each day—every decision, reaction, what we eat, how we move, how we speak to ourselves and others—is a program run by our subconscious mind. This is why we can consciously say "I want to be more patient," but as soon as a stressful situation arises, there we are, heart rate up, angry, and impatient. Or we say, "I want to start an exercise routine" and once again find ourselves scrolling on the phone.

Meditating will be the access into that subconscious programming. You'll be able to, on a deeper level, foster positive change and form new habits and patterns.

I am by no means an expert on meditation. I'm just dipping my toes into the vast ocean of methods, styles, breathing techniques, mantras, and visualizations that can be part of the practice. I recommend the wonderful book by Dr. Joe Dispenza, *Breaking the Habit of Being Yourself* for in depth benefits and methods.

But for now, literally all you need is five minutes and a quiet and comfortable place to sit.

Start by sitting with straight posture. Eyes closed and hands comfortably in your lap. Focus on your breathing. Breathing is the bridge to your subconscious mind. It's the only mechanism that is governed by your autonomic nervous system that you can control consciously as well.

Take a few deep, slow breaths, letting your belly expand on the inhale, to center yourself. Then let your focus rest on your body.

Relax each body part, top down, one at a time, with every exhale. Top of the head, all the muscles in your face, neck, chest, torso, arms, waist, bottom, thighs, calves, and feet. Feel your body relax and sink into the chair.

Then bring your awareness to where your body is in physical space. I like to start by picturing myself in the room I'm in and then zoom out like a GPS map, picturing the building, then the streets, then rivers, lakes and mountains, then oceans and continents, then the earth itself.

While your consciousness is now in the stratosphere looking down on beautiful planet earth, picture a giant cosmic movie screen. On that screen, show images of what your life would look like having achieved all your goals. Ideal weight, job, relationships, bank account. Show everything you wish to accomplish and achieve in vivid color and sound. Take as long as you want in this step.

Then bring to your awareness to one or two habits you wish to break. The ones keeping you from your ideal life. Don't judge or be harsh on yourself. Simply see them and mark them so that they never slip by in an unconscious program again.

Then one more time, quickly visualize yourself as having your ideal life. See yourself catching and correcting, in actual time, the habits holding you back. Visualize with all your senses your ideal life.

Then zoom back in from the atmosphere to your body. Take a second to stretch and move around. Gently open your eyes and start living your life as if nothing can stop you from achieving your goals.

If your mind wanders during meditation, just bring your attention back to your breath and refocus. This will inevitably happen. Don't think you're doing it wrong. It's very normal to drift from thought to thought. The more you can bring yourself back, the better you'll become at the practice. Every time your mind wanders and you bring it back is like a rep in an exercise routine. This refocusing is the work. It's where a lot of those benefits listed will come from.

Speaking from my own experience, the rewards of this practice are many. I will share a few of the habits and the unconscious programming that have held me back from my ideal self.

First and most importantly was and is impatience with my sweet, innocent children when they are just being their authentic selves—loud, rambunctious, wild, and sometimes downright dangerous. I could consciously tell myself that when my son is belting out a song and flailing about while my wife and I are trying to have a conversation, he's just a happy kid expressing joy, enjoying one of his loves, music. When I step back, this behavior is a very good thing actually. However, in that second when my wife and I can't hear each other, my reaction is something like, "HEY, bro, me and Mom are trying to talk here! Settle down, man." The joy leaves his face, and shame sinks into my soul for squashing childlike innocence. Pattern. Repeat. Slowly crushing the souls of my beautiful children and feeling terrible about it. A serious problem.

When I started meditating and picturing the habits I wish to break, this was the first I worked on. Something magical happens when you're in a meditative state and mark a behavior you wish to change. The first sign it's working is as you go to play the program you become aware, in actual time, of what's about to happen. In that moment with the particular program of being impatient, I was left confused and stuttering but not lashing out. Then I'd attempt a better way of communicating. Huge win.

As I would work on this bad program, I would picture myself gently walking into the next room where my son is singing loudly and dancing wildly during an important conversation attempted by my wife and me. In this ideal self-visualization, my reaction would go something like, "Hey bud, I love that you're so happy—sounds good, by the way. Is that Post Malone? Cool! So my guy, Mom and I are talking about all our awesome plans for this week. Can you take the concert up to your room for a few? Or maybe just work on the dance part for a minute? Cool! Love you, buddy."

As I continue to meditate and picture my ideal self, it deepens my ability to be that man. As I picture the ugliness of the impatience program, marking it to never slip by unconsciously, I become more and more consciously aware of my reaction.

I can say I'm not perfect. Very far from it. However, I can also say that there is a marked change in my ability to be kind and patient with my children in stressful situations thanks to my meditation practice.

The other examples of bad subconscious programming I've been successful in rewiring are road rage and unconscious eating while standing in front of the pantry.

Same thing! Picture ideal self, mark the bad programming so it can't sneak by automatically, picture ideal self again…and boom!

Now I go to the pantry to get a snack for my kids, the hand reaches for an Oreo, and the brain says, "Hold up! This is not congruent with your ideal self!" I pull the hand back.

Someone is driving fifty-two miles an hour in the passing lane while texting, so I am forced to pass them on the right, and as I do, they drift into my lane causing me to slam on the breaks. I then fly into a rage. Cortisol and adrenaline flood my body as I white knuckle grip the wheel and rant profanity laden half sentences. The texting driver carries on unaware of my vitriol. It is I left with the stress, anger, and shame of my reaction. What a waste of energy and an unnecessary dump of stress hormones.

Now, with meditation, I simply drive on safely, reminding myself that I most likely have also done whatever the other motorist is doing that is bothering me. No judgment. Just a quick prayer for their safety...most of the time. Hey! I'm still a work in progress.

These improvements actually happened pretty fast too. It started by being way more aware, in the moment, of my subconscious patterns. This happened after my first few times practicing meditation.

I know you can have similar results and have them quickly. Just wade in and try. There are courses, books, guided meditation videos on YouTube, and many other helpful resources to get you started.

You can also do meditative things like walking and focusing on breathing, sitting by the ocean and staring at the farthest point on the horizon, prayer, or enjoying a gratitude rampage (as named by Jack Canfield) where you rapid-fire name out loud things that you're grateful for, big and small, or you can lie in the grass connected to the earth and its magnetic electric charge. This is a process called grounding that has many physical and mental health benefits as well. Do this in conjunction or simultaneously with meditation to really amp up the benefits.

10

THE BEGINNING

Though we've come to the end of this book, it's really the beginning of something amazing. You are setting in motion thoughts, ideas, and actions that will change the trajectory of your life. Make this a turning point. A few degrees in a better direction spread out over a long distance and over time has a serious compounding effect. You will go to incredible new places.

For example, a jet leaving LAX for Boston has a set heading and trajectory. If you change the heading (the direction the nose of the plane is facing) just a few degrees south from that same starting point and travel the same 3,000 miles, you'll end up in Atlanta instead of Boston. That's the power of a few small changes over time and distance.

Take just one of the ideas from this book and change your heading. Start now. The sooner you do, the more dramatic the compounding will be.

I know you want positive change in your life. The fact you've read this far and still have the book in your hand is testament to that. I also know you are more than just ready. You are capable! Your success is around the corner. Pour yourself into your goals, and it's all but accomplished.

It sounds crazy, but the best way to help your friends, family, community, and world is to help yourself. When you fly on a plane, the flight attendant always demonstrates how to attach the oxygen mask and states that you should secure your mask *before* helping others. There is a fundamental truth in that small analogy. You need to be taken care of to effectively fulfill the needs of others.

Improving your life will have a ripple effect on the world around you. You will inevitably inspire others. Take that seriously. Be a role model for those you love— to all that you encounter. Glow and resonate positive energy. You'll be amazed at what the world gives you in return.

Now go off into this wonderful existence and improve yourself, mind, body, and spirit, each day. Serve others more effectively with the new and improved you. Be joyful and express gratitude. Put your best self forward, and you're already a success.

ABOUT THE AUTHOR

Anthony Snowdale is a national board-certified Integrative Health Practitioner (AADP), renowned personal trainer, and health and wellness coach. His passion for health and wellness extends to his personal life as a lifelong martial artist. Beyond the wellness sphere, Anthony is a successful real estate investor based on Boston's south shore. His achievements are not only professional but also personal, being a dedicated husband and father of two. His holistic approach to well-being and wealth forms the heart of his book, *Put Your Best Self Forward*. His life and work embody his belief in the power of positive change.

www.ingramcontent.com/pod-product-compliance
Lightning Source LLC
LaVergne TN
LVHW051957060526
838201LV00059B/3698